EAT   EAT   EAT   HA
HAGGIS   HAGGIS   HAGGIS   A
AND   AND   AND
CEILIDH   H   CEIL
ON   O.

EAT   EAT   EAT
HAGGIS   HAGGIS   HAGGIS
AND   AND   AND
CEILIDH   CEILIDH   CEILIDH   C
ON   ON   ON

EAT   EAT   EAT
HAGGIS   HAGGIS   HAGGIS   HA
AND   AND   AND   A
CEILIDH   CEILIDH   CEILIDH   CEIL
ON   ON   ON   O.

EAT   EAT   EAT
HAGGIS   HAGGIS   HAGGIS
AND   AND   AND
CEILIDH   CEILIDH   CEILIDH   . O
ON   ON   ON

EAT HAGGIS AND CEILIDH ON
EAT HAGGIS AND CEILIDH ON
EAT HAGGIS AND CEILIDH ON
EAT HAGGIS AND CEILIDH ON

EAT HAGGIS AND CEILIDH ON
EAT HAGGIS AND CEILIDH ON
EAT HAGGIS AND CEILIDH ON
HAGGIS AND CEILIDH ON

EAT HAGGIS AND CEILIDH ON
EAT HAGGIS AND CEILIDH ON
EAT HAGGIS AND CEILIDH ON
EAT HAGGIS AND CEILIDH ON

EAT HAGGIS AND CEILIDH ON
EAT HAGGIS AND CEILIDH ON
EAT HAGGIS AND CEILIDH ON
HAGGIS AND CEILIDH ON

EAT
HAGGIS
AND
CEILIDH
ON

EAT HAGGIS AND CEILIDH ON

Published by doodlemacdoodle in association with Summersdale

Bookspeed, 16 Salamander Yards, Edinburgh EH6 7DD
Tel: 0131 467 8100
Fax: 0131 467 8008
sales@bookspeed.com
www.bookspeed.com

Printed and bound in the Czech Republic

ISBN: 978-1-908661-00-5

Disclaimer
Every effort has been made to attribute the quotations in this
collection to the correct source. Should there be any omissions or
errors in this respect we apologise and shall be pleased to make the
appropriate acknowledgements in any future edition.

EAT
HAGGIS
AND
CEILIDH
ON

bookspeed

Scotland is the country above all others that I have seen, in which a man of imagination may carve out his own pleasures; there are so many *inhabited* solitudes.

Dorothy Wordsworth

Warm sandstone
tenement buildings.

Generally speaking,
the errors in religion
are dangerous; those in
philosophy only ridiculous.

David Hume

Making it to the top
of your first Munro –
with 282 more
to climb.

Scotland: where 'How?' means 'Why?'

Who indeed that has once
seen Edinburgh, but must
see it again in dreams
waking or sleeping?

Charlotte Brontë

Convictions start small.

(All our convictions were once whims.)

Proverb

**A million puffins
arrive in Scotland
every year to breed.**

Glasgow – aka The Green City – with over 90 public parks.

Discretion is being able to
raise your eyebrow instead
of your voice.

Sir Walter Scott

From rising to sleeping
Spinning and weaving
Words in a garment
Loose around my life
Talking and singing
Eating and meeting
Such is the ceilidh
The joy of my life.

Robert Urquhart,
The Ceilidh Place, Ullapool

'Ceilidh' can mean
a party, a concert,
or more usually an
evening of informal
Scottish traditional
dancing.

Biting into a
Tunnock's Teacake
and then smoothing
out the silver foil.

Oats. A grain which in England is generally given to horses, but in Scotland supports the people.

Dr Johnson

The loch's slopes glow gold
from sun on spent,
wet bracken.
Along the edge, a rowan's
leaves return the gold and,
With berries like beacons,
It sways,
As true a flag as any Saltire.

Anonymous, 'Autumn in Scotland'

Thinking about
landing in a seaplane
on Loch Lomond or
Oban Harbour.

The signing of the
Auld Alliance in
1295 gave the Scots
French support
against England, and
also gave us the first
choice of Bordeaux's
finest wines.

If that you will France win,
Then with Scotland
first begin.

William Shakespeare, *Henry V*

She's goat mair
degrees than a
thermometer.

(She's very clever.)

Senga and Agnes, the Scottish Twins.

Whisky porridge, left overnight to soak.

They talk of my drinking but
never my thirst.

Proverb

The one haunting and
exasperatingly loveable city
in Scotland.

Lewis Grassic Gibbon
on Aberdeen

Playing golf at
midnight in Kirkwall
at the summer solstice.

The Falkirk Wheel,
a symbol of Scottish
innovation and
ingenuity, the world's
first rotating boat lift.

I just think the most difficult
thing to displace is privilege.

Sean Connery

I wish to have no connection with any ship that does not sail fast, for I intend to go in harm's way.

John Paul Jones, once a disgraced Scottish sailor, who became known as the founder of the US Navy

Crossing the
Forth Bridge by
train – and hearing
everything rattle.

**Feeling and seeing the
final movement of the
Festival Fireworks.**

Earthquake House, Comrie, one of the oldest permanent seismic observatories. Lying on the Highland Boundary Fault, Comrie is also known as the 'Shakin' Toon'.

The texture and
waterproof qualities
of Harris Tweed – the
only cloth in the world
protected by an act
of parliament.

Dae weel and hae luck.

(Make your own luck.)

Proverb

Palm trees on the Isle of Arran, Plockton, Inverewe and all along the West Coast.

The Enchanted Forest
near Pitlochry.

Self-rule for Scotland would
make us grow up.

Alasdair Gray

Listening to (and paying) the piper at Carter Bar when arriving in Scotland on the A68.

Wishing everybody
you meet 'Happy
New Year' for days,
weeks and sometimes
months.

The imagination is not an
escape, but a return to the
richness of our true selves;
a return to reality.

George Mackay Brown

There's aye a
something.

(Accepting adversity.)

Renewable energy:
Scotland has an
estimated potential of
36.5 GW of wind and
7.5 GW of tidal energy,
25% of the total
European capacity.

Salt 'n' sauce.

(On your chips.)

The smell of
the old Glasgow
Underground.

There are some people who
say that the English are not
ready to govern themselves,
but I think they are.

Alex Salmond

Ice climbing on Point
Five Gully on the first
of May on Ben Nevis.

Winning the second
half of the quarter
final of the 1999
Rugby World Cup at
Murrayfield against
the All Blacks... but
losing the match
18–30.

Melrose Sevens, the oldest and most famous rugby sevens competition, dating from 1883. The 2011 winners were... Melrose RFC!

Ceilidh – always means having a good time.

Pit mair in than ye tak oot.

Proverb

Beatrix Potter wrote *The Tale of Peter Rabbit* **when holidaying in Birnam in 1893.**

Autumn colours
around Birnam
and Dunkeld.

Auld Scotland wants nae
skinking ware
That jaups in luggies;
But, if you wish her
gratefu' prayer
Gie her a Haggis.

**Rabbie Burns,
'Address to a Haggis'**

'Gentle Johnny'
Ramensky – criminal,
war hero and master
of escape.

Playing kerby with
a friend, a football,
a road and two
pavements.

We never lost a game; we
just ran out of time.

Sir Alex Ferguson

They that will not be
counselled cannot
be helped.

Proverb

The Scots have been
drinking claret since
1295, when the Auld
Alliance was signed. It
was landed in Leith on
Wine Quay.

51 National Nature
Reserves.

Flying Scotsmen: the dance, the train and the cyclists.

We have most of our
celebrations in the
coldest part of
the year.

I prefer to stay home with
fish fingers and a book
at Christmas.

Donald Dewar

Bagpipes, traditionally made from entire animal pelts, such as goats, dogs, sheep and cows, are now more likely to be made from synthetics, including Gore-Tex.

Electronic bagpipes – played online and elsewhere – with no animal pelts, Gore-Tex, or any bag or bellows at all. Funky!

For everybody knows that it
requires very little to satisfy
the gentlemen, if a woman
will only give her mind to it.

Margaret Oliphant

The first wheeze of
the accordion at
the start of each
ceilidh dance.

Paisley, the home of Marion Robertson's 'Golden Shred' marmalade.

The Boys' Brigade,
They are afraid,
To stick their nose
In marmalade.

Playground rhyme

We do have the greatest
fans in the world but I've
never yet seen a fan
score a goal.

Jock Stein

Scottish wood ants
build mound nests
up to three metres
in circumference,
one metre in height,
and contain 100,000
workers and several
queen ants.

Seeing the Northern
Lights from as far
south as Dunbar.

Every year my heart
becomes more fixed on this
dear pasture.

Queen Victoria on Royal Deeside

Seawater in Mallaig
which is clearer than
the Caribbean, and
sand which is whiter.

Going 'doon the
watter' on the Clyde,
aboard the Waverley
Paddle Steamer.

Sir Robert the Bruce at
Bannockburn
Beat the English in every
wheel and turn,
And made them fly in
great dismay
From off the field
without delay.

**William McGonagall,
'The Battle of Bannockburn'**

The MacBean tartan
was taken to the moon
by US astronaut Alan
Bean in 1969 (but he
didn't leave it there).

Alexandria, Argyll
– home of the first
purpose-built car
factory in the UK,
constructed in 1906.

Charles Macintosh, the Glaswegian chemist, patented waterproof material in 1823 and his first 'mac' went on sale the following year.

Caledonian
MacBrayne ferries,
in their red and
black livery, sailing
backwards and
forwards all along
the West Coast.

There are as good fish in
the sea as ever came
out of it.

Sir Walter Scott

The Leith police dismisseth us
They thought we sought to stay;
The Leith police dismisseth us
They thought we'd stay all day.
The Leith police dismisseth us,
We both sighed sighs apiece;
And the sighs that we sighed
as we said goodbye
Were the size of the Leith police.

Leith Tongue Twister

The official heraldic
animal of Scotland is
the unicorn.

The incredibly ornate
Italian Chapel built
by prisoners of war
in Orkney while
constructing the
Churchill barriers to
keep out the U-boats
in World War Two.

Ambition's a great seed.

Proverb

In the end is my beginning.

Mary Queen of Scots

790 islands of which
130 are inhabited.

Edinburgh was the
first city in the world
to have its own fire
brigade – founded
in 1824.

14,000 Scots identified themselves as 'Jedi' in the 2001 census.

The Apple Tree Gang, and John Reid in particular – often described as 'the father of American golf' – founded the St Andrew's Golf Club in Yonkers in 1888.

Always try to set the heather on fire.

(Always try to do well.)

Proverb

**Mohammed is now
one of the top 100
names for Scots boys.**

Christmas Day only
became a public
holiday in Scotland
in 1958.

I have brought you to the
ring and now you
must dance.

William Wallace

Wally Closes: Glasgow tenement entrances decorated with ceramic tiles.

The Unst Bus Shelter, Shetland. Famous for hamsters, weapons inspectors and the John Peel Memorial Traffic Island.

Tobermory *is*
Balamory.

Wet sheep don't shrink – they shake off the water.

(Don't give in to misfortune.)

Proverb

**Kilmahog in the
Trossachs: a fabled
tradition of dressing
up as pigs on 1 April,
to outwit the Devil.**

Great films directed by Bill Forsyth: *That Sinking Feeling, Gregory's Girl* and *Local Hero.*

David Niven –
Kirriemuir-born
actor regarded
as the archetypal
Englishman!

T in the Park
music festival.

There are two kinds of artists left: those who endorse Pepsi and those who simply won't.

Annie Lennox

Laphroaig: the
celebrated Islay malt
whisky with a smoky
seaweedy flavour – an
'acquired' taste.

Hot toddy: a great remedy for the common cold containing heather honey, whisky and boiling water stirred with a silver spoon.

Mary had a little lamb,
Its fleece was slightly grey,
It didn't have a father,
Just some borrowed DNA.

Joke celebrating Dolly the sheep

7,000,000 sheep
in Scotland.

Salmon remember the
smell of their 'home'
stream – even after
four years at sea.

The largest salmon
ever caught by fishing
rod in the UK was
landed by Georgina
Ballantyne on the
River Tay in 1922. It
weighed 64lb!

Better do it than wish it.

Proverb

**Great Britain won
the Gold Medal for
women's curling at the
2002 Winter Olympics
– but the team was
all Scottish!**

I think I'm going back
to California... in
West Lothian.

Only dead salmon swim
with the current.

Proverb

Camping right on the edge of Loch Tummel by the Queen's View at Loch Tummel Caravan Park.

**Scotland's fresh
water lochs cover
600 square miles.**

Ebenezer Place, Wick, is the shortest street in the world. It was built in 1883, measures only 81 inches and contains only one address.

A propensity to hope and
joy is real riches; one to fear
and sorrow real poverty.

David Hume

Jelly on the plate,
Jelly on the plate
Wiggle, waggle,
Wiggle, waggle
Jelly on the plate.

Children's verse

Mackie's Ice Cream, made in Aberdeenshire, is carbon neutral and produced completely by wind power.

Strathkinness cheese
is Scotland's answer
to Gruyère; rich in
protein, it tastes great
with crusty bread
or oatcakes.

The best thing in life is to
mak the maist o't that
we can.

James Hogg

The Meikleour Beech
Hedge, on the A93
Perth–Blairgowrie
Road, planted in
1745, is the tallest and
longest hedge in the
world; 100ft high and
1/3 mile long.

**The Fortingall Yew
(*Taxus baccata*): over
5,000 years old and the
oldest living thing
in Europe.**

French and Scots
citizens born before
1906 had dual
nationality of the
two countries.

Scotland has an in-built
sound system that never
stops thumping.

KT Tunstall

There is scarce a deep sea
light from the Isle of Man to
North Berwick, but one of
my blood designed it.

Robert Louis Stevenson,
Memoirs of Himself

The darkest skies in
Europe can be seen
at the Galloway Dark
Sky Park.

Scotland's Secret
Bunker: listen to the
sirens on the website
before you even
go there.

Keep a calm sooch.

(Keep calm/hold your tongue.)

The truth springs from
arguments amongst friends.

David Hume

The founding principles of the Scottish Parliament: power sharing, accountability, access and participation, equal opportunity.

Travelling up the A9
through Perth, over
Drumochter, Slochd
and on to Inverness.

Nothing is more surprising
than the easiness with which
the many are governed
by the few.

David Hume

Timor mortis
conturbat me.

*(The fear of death
perturbs me.)*

**William Dunbar,
'The Lament for the Makars'**

The Loony Dook and Ne'erday (New Year's Day) swims in the super-cold seas all around the coast.

Ospreys, after decades
of apparent absence,
returned to breed
in Scotland during
the 1950s, and their
population has now
reached over 200 pairs.

Ane at a time is guid fishing.

(Be content with your life.)

Proverb

Some hae meat
and canna eat,
And some wad eat
that want it,
But we hae meat
and we can eat,
and sae the Lord be thankit.

Rabbie Burns, 'The Selkirk Grace'

Belted Galloway
cattle, primarily
raised for their high-
quality, marbled beef,
although sometimes
milked and stocked
just to adorn the
fields with their
fabulous stripe.

'Ceilidh' derives
from the Gaelic word
meaning 'a visit'.

The Gay Gordons –
not only a Scottish
country dance,
but also a game
of patience.

Stonehaven's unique
Olympic-sized heated
outdoor seawater
swimming pool – in
an Art Deco listed
building.

O wad some Pow'r the giftie
gie us
To see oursels as others
see us

Rabbie Burns, 'To a Louse'

I paint myself because I
am available and I am the
cheapest model I know.

Jack Vettriano

Karl Marx was
supposed to have
been a passenger on
the train that crashed
during the Tay Bridge
Disaster but cancelled
his journey due
to illness.

**Arbroath Smokie:
a wood-smoked
haddock still
produced in small
family smoke-houses
in Arbroath on the
east coast of Scotland.**

Just exactly what is Irn Bru made from…?

He liked to play his
bagpipes up and down, and
that was how he brought us
out of town.

Geoffrey Chaucer on the Miller,
The Canterbury Tales

'Pinkie', the Scots
word for 'little finger',
was given to us by
Flemish traders.

The never-failing
excitement of travelling
through Glencoe.

**Morris Harrison, the very best
Scottish salesman**

Every line of strength in American history is a line coloured with Scottish blood.

**Woodrow Wilson,
28th President of the USA**

Reading and sauntering
and lounging and dosing,
which I call thinking, is my
supreme happiness.

David Hume

Cromarty, southeast veering south or southwest, 5 to 7, perhaps gale 8 for a time later, decreasing 4 or 5 later.

What's the Point
of Ardnamurchan?
A great place for a
Viking ship burial.

I only went out for a walk,
and finally concluded to stay
out till sundown, for going
out, I found, was really
going in.

John Muir

To be kind to all, to like many and love a few, to be needed and wanted by those we love, is certainly the nearest we can come to happiness.

Mary I of Scotland

The world is neither
Scottish, English, nor Irish,
neither French, Dutch, nor
Chinese, but human.

James Grant

OCH
WHEESHT
AND
GET OAN
WAE IT

OCH WHEESHT AND GET OAN WAE IT

£4.99

Hardback

ISBN: 978-0-95536-411-2

WHIT'S FUR YE'LL NO GO BY YE!

Timeless Scottish wisdom
for every occasion

www.bookspeed.com

Eat Haggis and Ceilidh On is the second book
in the 'Dynamic Words from Scotland' series,
published by **doodlemacdoodle**. Also available:
Och Wheesht and Get Oan Wae It.

For other related 'Eat Haggis and Ceilidh On'
products, including mugs, T-shirts and cards,
please visit

www.eathaggis.com

EAT
HAGGIS
AND
CEILIDH
ON

EAT
HAGGIS
AND
CEILIDH
ON

EAT
HAGGIS
AND
CEILIDH
ON

HA
CEIL
O

EAT
HAGGIS
AND
CEILIDH
ON

EAT
HAGGIS
AND
CEILIDH
ON

EAT
HAGGIS
AND
CEILIDH
ON

EAT
HAGGIS
AND
CEILIDH
ON

EAT
HAGGIS
AND
CEILIDH
ON

EAT
HAGGIS
AND
CEILIDH
ON

HA
CEIL
O

EAT
HAGGIS
AND
CEILIDH
ON

EAT
HAGGIS
AND
CEILIDH
ON

EAT
HAGGIS
AND
CEILIDH
ON

EAT HAGGIS AND CEILIDH ON